LOVE HIM

ISBN: 9798571147521

A publication of Tall Pine Books

|| tallpinebooks.com

*Printed in the United States of America

LOVE HIM

HE LIVES WHERE HE IS LOVED

ERIC GILMOUR

"Sitting at the feet of Jesus
Oh, what words I hear Him say!
Happy place! so near, so precious!
May it find me there each day
Sitting at the feet of Jesus
I would look upon the past
For His love has been so gracious
It has won my heart at last
Sitting at the feet of Jesus
Where can mortal be more blest?
There I lay my sins and sorrows
And, when weary, find sweet rest
Sitting at the feet of Jesus
There I love to weep and pray
While I, from His fullness, gather
Grace and comfort every day
Bless me, O my Savior, bless me
As I sit low at Thy feet
Oh, look down in love upon me
Let me see Thy face so sweet
Give me, Lord, the mind of Jesus
Keep me holy, as He is
May I prove I've been with Jesus
Who is all my righteousness"
—Ernie Haase

"We have one thing on our hearts—it is You. You're all that matters. Heaven and earth shall pass away, but You and Your words, shall live forever. Now, my Love, I ask You to whisper in our ears. As we lay our head upon Your chest, I pray we would gain access to the divine treasure chest. May we see Jesus as the riches, and endless treasure divine. In your holy name, amen."

I write to pluck the strings of your heart. I write not with a hammer to dash you, nor a whip to flog you, but with a honeycomb to exhilarate your heart with the taste of Christ. Oh, that we would taste Him, again and again, as our daily life supply. You may say, "I've already tasted." Then you ought to be the most excited about tasting Him again. I am constantly praying to the Holy Spirit, "Give me the voice of the Bridegroom." This is most important to me when I am preaching or when writing. One day, I felt the Lord speak to my heart through my nine-year-old daughter while I was playing Barbies with her. She was spontaneously dialoguing between two Barbies. One said to the other, "Girls don't want to be yelled at when they're being proposed to." I thought that it was brilliant! Jesus is always so tender. His voice is like tranquil, passionate love-whispers that break bones.

As you read this, look upon Christ the Bridegroom. Together, let's adore Him and simply leave ourselves there without that human itch to move on to something lesser. Let's just abandon everything else and give ourselves and everything that has to do with us over to Him. I must make another note upon a love relationship with the Bridegroom. Such an exchange is inseparable from joy. Without joy, God is misrepresented. I see some people preaching the gospel sometimes and they're so mad. I think to myself, *Don't they know it's good news? Glad tidings of great joy?* For, as the hymn states: "His law is love and His gospel is peace."

"JESUS IS EVERYTHING, SO HE CAN'T BE A PART OF ANYTHING."

Recently, I had a dream. A very special person whom I highly respect as a man of God came to me and said, "Hey, do you want to know the secret of union with God?" I said, "Yeah, I do." He then grabbed me and he pulled me into a room away from everybody else. He shut the door. I leaned in to hear these amazing words of wisdom that would reveal to me the secret.

He then simply opened his mouth and softly and intimately sang, "Jesus, I love You. Jesus, I love You. Jesus, I love You." He completely forgot about me. He even forgot about himself. He continued, "Jesus, I love You." When I woke from the dream, I thought to myself, *You know, he never told me the special secret.* Then I realized he was *exemplifying* the secret for me. It was...

1. Getting away from people,
2. Shutting the door
3. Forgetting yourself
4. Forgetting everyone else
5. Simply lifting your heart in tender *love to Christ.*

That's the mark. It is tragic to admit but I feel that, sometimes, we want something more than that. Yet there just isn't anything more than to love Him. Because in loving Him, we receive Him. He is everything. The eternal object of love. My friend Michael Koulianos likes to say, "Jesus is everything, so He can't be a part of anything." He is all of it.

"AT TIMES, OUR LANGUAGE IS RIGHT BUT OUR HEART IS
NUMB."

With this, I want to write specifically on love and marriage. They go together like a horse and carriage. This, I tell you, brother: you can't have one without the other. Bridal language must be accompanied by bridal love. When we talk about marriage (commitment) to Him, we must not lose sweet love-exchange with Him. At times, our language is right but our heart is numb. The language is electric but the heart is stale. The Lord wants to constantly renew the love in each one of our hearts. I feel that this writing is an invitation into a deeper *feeling*. I say that word *feeling* without any shame. People push feelings away. How can we separate love and affection?

It bothers me when people say things like, *"You know, you can't expect feelings."* Wait, does the Holy Spirit give me love, joy and peace? Are these not the undeniable fruit of the Spirit's root in my life? These *are felt*. Is anyone interested in a peace they cannot feel? Do you want a joy that you don't feel? It doesn't make any sense. Jesus named the Holy Spirit "The Comforter." Are these restricted to theological consolations? Are they not actual consolations from a living person? As Paul states, with great emphasis, *"Therefore if there is any encouragement in Christ, if there is any consolation of love, if there is any fellowship of the Spirit, if any affection and compassion, make my joy complete by being of the same mind, maintaining the same love, united in spirit, intent on one purpose."*

"WHAT'S MORE IMPORTANT? BREATHING IN OR
BREATHING OUT?"

He wants our love. Our hearts are His prize. I can sense the Lord longing for our highest love. *"Do you love Me more than these?"* Jesus asks in John 21:15. He has asked me this many times. I travel a lot and I go to places and I miss my family. I miss my wife. I love being with my wife, my best friend. My kids weep sometimes when I leave. Sometimes, in service to the Lord and obedience to my call, I miss special things that I will never be able to be experienced again.

At times, my heart hurts and I want to go home. But when I am feeling this way, I begin to lose myself in worship. He seems to come to me and show me my daughters. He shows me my wife. I see them like a movie. It almost feels real. And then He whispers in my ear, *"Do you love Me more than these?"* And I have to open my heart and look deep inside and see if I have an idol. When my heart settles and I say, "Yes, I do, Lord. Yes I do." He takes my heart up into Himself. Highest love reaches the highest places.

There is One more precious to me
More precious than family,
Liberty, heritage or history,
Someone who's more precious than prosperity
And victory
It is Him who is in me
Lord, there's no light to dim Thee
No effort could ever win Thee
You give Yourself freely.
I give my soul to Thee.

"The Lord keeps all who love Him." (Psalm 145:20)

That's the essence of what marriage is. We love His presence and His words. I don't understand people who say things like, "What's more important? The Bible or the presence?" When somebody once asked Charles Spurgeon this question, he replied, *"What's more important? Breathing in or breathing out?"* We love Him and His voice. We love His voice and Him.

It's simple and so straightforward—a child will understand it. Sometimes, people want to put an asterisk there, as if to say, *"The Lord keeps all who love Him* but...."* You can't add a disclaimer. The language is clear as day. *"The Lord keeps all who love Him."* This means that our job is not to keep ourselves. Our job is to love Him. And when we give more of our time to *keeping* than *loving*, it's no wonder we're not kept. You don't need to keep yourself. You love Him and He will keep you. That's the key.

If I took you to a bunch of homeless people, turned you over to them and said, "They're going to take care of you," they wouldn't be able to do much for you. They don't have anything. The poor can only give poverty. But if I turned you over to a loyal, kind, wealthy family, they could help you in some way. They have something. Those who are rich have much to give. But when you love God, you're turned over to the eternal-limitless, paternal God of love. He can infinitely protect and keep you.

"LIVE IN THE ABSOLUTE DEPENDENCE OF ONE WHO CAN DO NOTHING."

You would feel really safe if you saw a security guard nearby. You would feel a bit safer if you had a personal guard designated for you. How much safer would you feel if you had a garrison—a whole army in front of you? But even these images are inferior to having God as your keeper. *"The Lord keeps all who love Him."* I feel like we need a fresh understanding of what Andrew Murray said: "Live in the absolute dependence of one who can do nothing." When we realize that we're unable to do anything, we discover what real joy is. There isn't a greater joy than truly believing that there's nothing we can do, and that we can actually trust Him to do everything. That's when you're free to actually be happy. It's all your effort, your resolve and your determination that get in your way. Self-consciousness is man's disease.

It's better just to relinquish everything and trust Him and love Him. A. W. Tozer says, "The man who has struggled to purify himself and has had nothing but repeated failures will experience real relief when he stops tinkering with his soul and looks away to the perfect One." He goes on to say, "While he looks at Christ the very thing he has so long been trying to do will be getting done within him. It will be God working in him to will and to do." God is able to work on the inside of us. In surrender, you accomplish more by accident than you ever did on purpose. *"It is God who works in you both to will and to do for His good pleasure"* (Philippians 2:13).

Learning the spiritual life is full of sweetness. I don't know anybody who's perfected it. Everybody's learning it, but the Lord takes on the responsibility of keeping you.

"LET YOUR *EVERY DAY* BE FOCUSED ON YOUR *HEART-LOVE EXCHANGE WITH JESUS.*"

If you just just keep your love on Him as your one goal, He will perfect that which concerns you. If I leave you with anything in this book, may it be this: let your *every day* be focused on your *heart-love exchange with Jesus*. That's it. In this, we will find that all the things in our lives begin to work together for our good, because the Bible tells us that all things work together for the good to *those who love Him.* (See Romans 8:28.)

So as you love Him, He arranges everything. Even the stuff that looks like it's terrible and it's not right. Read this closely, even the stuff that looks wrong. When you look away to the Lord and are directly connected with Him, you will begin to see that His providence is perfect. One man of God noted that "the providence of God is like Hebrew words--it can only be read backwards." So you don't realize His providence in the moment, but when you look back, you can see His perfections. Perhaps someone is bothering you at your job. Yet, without you realizing it, you will one day look back and say, "Oh, how that all served me and worked together for my good."

Andrew Murray's masterpiece of a quote would fit well here: "Let us look on every brother or sister who tries or vexes us as God's means of grace, God's instrument for our purification, for our exercise of the humility Jesus our Life breathes within us."

If something causes you to draw nearer to the Lord, then you have a greater gain than anything you could have ever lost. Surrendering to Him is the glad, joyous, willing response of love upon love.

"THE ONE WHO HAS MY COMMANDMENTS AND KEEPS THEM IS THE ONE WHO LOVES ME; AND THE ONE WHO LOVES ME WILL BE LOVED BY MY FATHER, AND I WILL LOVE HIM AND WILL DISCLOSE MYSELF TO HIM." (JOHN 14:21)

Do you see what happens when you love Him? You get a *disclosure*. This word actually means *"a personal appearance."* In other words, "If you love Me, you get personal appearances." There are people who go into their rooms and leave the same way they came in because they never *loved*. They never looked with adoration upon His beauty. They never worshipped at His feet. They may have done many things, but never once were their hearts crying, "Jesus, I love You."

This heart exchange is *everything*. There can be many types of methods and principles and devotions that people do, but lovers enter into communion with God alone. You see, God does not spread a table for principles. He spreads the table for those people who love Him. Then He lays Himself on the table as the meal. The self-disciplined people are proud of themselves. I've fallen into this in my life. Many times, you can become proud of your discipline. The only problem with this is that it is the opposite of love. Pride cannot love. Love cannot be proud. Devotion to our devotions is far from jealous desire for Him.

This is a problem because God only discloses Himself--literally, shows Himself--to those who love Him. He's made it this way because He is not looking for warriors or a crossfit champion. He's looking for a bride who receives her beauty from Him. He returns for the one who loves Him and comes out to meet Him with the oil of love. While the self-disciplined are proud of themselves, the lovers enjoy themselves.

"IF YOU WANT TO GO UP, YOU'VE GOT TO LET GO OF
THE THINGS BELOW."

It took me a long time to realize that the only thing God is looking for from me is the enjoyment of Him. Even today, I am constantly in need of the Spirit's remembrance of this truth. I thought there had to be more. I figured I would stumble upon enjoyment here and there. But one day, it clicked. The New Covenant, the whole thing, is *enjoyment of Christ.* Striving is the curse. When we realize this, we simply sit at the table and eat and enjoy.

Some people approach God as if He is a workout routine. Personally, I work out almost every day. And every day, I don't want to do it. Yet I do it because I know that I need to do it if I want to remain healthy. *That is not how prayer should be.* Brides don't go into the bridal chamber reluctantly. They run in. They desire Him. This book is a basket of rose petals to lead you to the King's chamber. When you begin to open the door to the King's chamber, the light rays from His face blind you to everything else.

"Six days later, Jesus took with Him Peter and James and John his brother, and led them up on a high mountain by themselves." (Matthew 17:1)

Are you seeing what's going on here? Jesus is already with them, and yet, Jesus takes them higher. As you read this, see Him with You, and yet, inviting you into something higher. He wants to show you something in the heights. Notice, when He leads them, He leads them up on a high mountain, which means they leave all of the things below. *When you go up, you leave the things below.* Here's the reason why a lot of people never go up: because they don't want to leave the things below.

"AND HE WAS TRANSFIGURED BEFORE THEM; AND HIS
FACE SHONE LIKE THE SUN, AND HIS GARMENTS
BECAME AS WHITE AS LIGHT." (MATTHEW 17:2)

Often, as Jesus is trying to take people up, they're grabbing on to something to remain below. However, if you want to go up, you've got to let go of the things below. As long as you want to hold on to the things below, you'll never go up. Can Jesus be with you in the midst of the things below? Yes, but He has something higher for you.

Again, Jesus is already with them, yet, He says, "I want to show you something. I've got a surprise for you." He takes them up high and they leave all things below. And at that high place, He reveals the surprise: *Himself*. He shows Himself. He is the prized surprise. All God's gifts are Jesus. You see, some people are hungry for God because they feel as if God is not giving them anything. "Throw me a bone, Lord." That's not hunger. This hunger is likened to a child opening Christmas presents. The child opens one and yearns with wide eyes, "I love this, but give me the next one, I'm hungry for the next one. And the next one after that!" God opens Himself to us again and again and again. This is the target of our hunger. So what is the word of the Lord to you right now? You're walking with Jesus, but He wants to show you something. Jesus is saying to you, "Let's leave these things, these people, these situations, and go up. I want to show you Me."

In this high place, God speaks from heaven, and it is the last time the sky rumbles and God Almighty gives a command into the earth. He says, *"This is My beloved Son, with whom I am well-pleased; listen to Him!"* (Matthew 17:5). In other words, "Pay attention to Him. Give Him all of your attention."

"YOU ARE NEVER MORE HUMBLE THAN WHEN YOU
ADORE JESUS."

Hebrews chapter 2 echoes this God-call from the sky, when the writer describes that, in times of old, God spoke through prophets, but now all of the attention is on Jesus. I believe that God has not stopped that commandment. It came forth and it lives forever. Hebrews 2:1 shows us that *"we must pay much closer attention* [to Christ]*...that we do not drift away."* To drift is easy; you don't do anything. If we pay attention to Christ, we will remain with Him.

"When the disciples heard this, they fell face down...." (Matthew 17:6)

The disciples' response to God's voice shows me that humility comes from seeing Jesus. Some people think that humility is thinking lower of yourself. No, humility is seeing the Lord. When you lift your eyes to the Lord, you're never more humble, for you are removed from the picture. See, if your head is up, it is not humility. If your head is down, it is not humility. Both are pride.

Whether you think yourself *something* or you think yourself *nothing*, it's still about you. But if you look at Jesus, if you adore Him, you forget yourself. You are never more humble than when you adore Jesus. And so these men fall on their faces because of a manifestation of the wonder and majesty of the person of Jesus. Humility is when your legs are broken by the weight of God's presence. When your eyes are blinded by His effulgence. When your breath is taken by His splendor.

"HYPOCRITES PRAY BENEATH A MASK."

We can't work on humility. We must bask in His beams and become streams. Some say, "I'm working on my humility." Well, good luck, my friend. Try your best. You're not going to be able to do it. Let me save you the suspense. You can't even love people. Just quit. Look at Jesus and let Him become love through you. "I'm working on my patience," others say. Listen, forget patience. Look at Jesus and He will become *patience* on the inside of you. This is the only way that pleases God.

Even if you were patient in yourself, it wouldn't please God, because He is only pleased with Jesus. This presents you with a problem, and it is a *wonderful* problem. You have to realize that you're nothing. Even your goodness couldn't be any more worthless. Oh, it's the best feeling in the world. *I can't even love You without You, Lord.* In this, you're free to be honest and live in total abandonment.

Some people go into the closet, and they wonder why they can't experience God's presence. It's because they are wearing a mask. Jesus says, *"When you pray, you are not to be like the hypocrites"* (Matthew 6:5). The word *hypocrite* means "interpreter from beneath." Hypocrites pray beneath a mask. In that day, stage actors would put on a mask and interpret from beneath a mask. So Jesus says, in effect, "When you come to pray, you can't bring your mask. You can't bring your mask into the closet."

In other words, some people go into the closet and they're not vulnerably honest. They're doing what they *think* they're supposed to do, and saying what they *feel* they need to say.

"I BELIEVE IN CHRISTIANITY AS I BELIEVE THAT THE
SUN HAS RISEN: NOT ONLY BECAUSE I SEE IT, BUT
BECAUSE BY IT I SEE EVERYTHING ELSE."

It's so much better to go in and be truthful in silence than to utter a bunch of empty words. Jesus says, "Don't do this. I don't want to hear your words if they're not from your heart."

This is the reason some people go into the bridal chamber and wonder, *Where is He?* He only manifests Himself to those who love Him. Many go into the closet wondering, *Where is He?* And you quickly realize that hell is summed up in this one question: *Where is He?* When you begin to just linger there, you soon find all that you need.

Exclusive attention leads to exclusive vision. When the disciples fell on their faces in the high place, the Bible goes on to say, *"And lifting up their eyes, they saw no one except Jesus Himself alone"* (Matthew 17:8). Isn't this wonderful? They saw nobody but Jesus. All the things that had held their attention in the past, they saw no more, because of a manifestation of Jesus. They only saw Him. He became the paradigm through which they now looked.

C.S. Lewis said, "I believe in Christianity as I believe that the sun has risen: not only because I see it, but because by it I see everything else." This is how we believe in Jesus. Not only can we see Him, but by Him, we see everything else. And without Him, we can't see anything at all. Without Him, we are lost in confusion.

"JESUS ANSWERED AND SAID TO HIM, 'IF ANYONE LOVES ME, HE WILL KEEP MY WORD; AND MY FATHER WILL LOVE HIM, AND WE WILL COME TO HIM AND MAKE OUR ABODE WITH HIM.'" (JOHN 14:23)

You have already seen that if you love Him, He is going to keep you. You already see that if you love Him, He will open your eyes. Now you see that if you love Him, He will live in you. You'll become a habitation for Him. *He only lives where He is loved.* That's why it's very difficult to sense the Lord when your heart starts growing stale. This is why the Scripture says, "Above all else, guard your heart" (see Proverbs 4:23), because if your heart starts getting messed up, everything goes wrong.

Scripture describes the heart as the spring from which flows all the streams of our lives. (See Proverbs 4:23.) Even our theology flows from our heart. This is the reason we have so much chaotic, crazy theology out there—if there is dirt in the spring, there is mud in the streams. If there's dirt in the root, it brings for bad fruit. Issues of the heart are the reasons why there are so many strange world paradigms. Yet, if the heart loves, then God dwells within. Some people have studied themselves out of love. God dwells not with them. Leonard Ravenhill once said, "We are not here to get to know the Word of God but to know the God of the Word."

Do I love the Scriptures? Beyond question—they're a daily life source for me. They are the window through which we look at the face of Jesus. Yet we can't study ourselves away from experience. The Bible is the blessed book of experience. We don't believe so that we understand. We believe that we may experience. This is the root and the key.

"IT'S ABOUT NESTLING, NOT WRESTLING."

There's a story of a boy who found a beautiful flower. He adored the flower and showed everybody its beauty. He loved it. He then thought to himself, *I want to understand this flower.* So he began to open the flower, dissect it, pulling off petal after petal. He was thinking about it deeply and logically, pulling it apart until there was nothing left to adore.

And so it is with so many people in their Christian lives. They begin adoring the Lord, and then they seek to explain and expound and understand; trying to apprehend God by logic. They pick God apart to the point that they have nothing left to adore. They study the beauty out of Jesus instead of worshipping the beauty of Jesus that the Scriptures reveal. I've seen this happen many times in my own life, becoming lost in mental traps of human reason. But the light of faith demands that a man transcend the scope of His own reason, finally giving up and saying, "Oh, Lord, only You know." I tearfully say to you that I do not want anything to do with defining Jesus at the cost of the sense of His presence. I want to keep my heart in love with Him. That is all.

Some people *strive* themselves out of faith. We need a faith that is strong enough to put an end to our effort. We have to recognize that when we set effort in motion, we are rejecting the righteousness that Jesus freely gives. Remember, Jesus is not just righteousness *for* us, He is righteousness *through* us. Righteousness in our lives is a result of yielding to Him. We find that the issues of our lives are not about what is forced out but what flows out as He flows in. It's not about duties but delight. Snuggling, not struggling. Nestling, not wrestling.

"WHEN WE LOVE HIM, WE TRUST HIM."

A child trusts its father because the child loves him. As you love God, you trust Him. If you have children, you know that your children love you and trust you. If my daughter had a choice to have me help her with something or have somebody else help her who was far better at that particular thing, she would still pick me because her love for me causes her to trust me. Her lack of love for the expert causes her not to trust him. So it is with God. When we love Him, we trust Him.

There was a man who pulled everyone in his city together and stretched a tightrope from one building to the other. He asked, "How many believe I can walk the tightrope from this building to that building?" Everyone expressed uncertainty. He walked across successfully, the crowds gasped. Again, he asked, "How many believe I can walk back?" By this point, everyone believed and shouted, "Yeah! Yeah!" So he did. He then asked, "How many believe I can walk across this while pushing a wheelbarrow?"

Everyone confidently shouted, "Yeah!" He replied, "Which one of you is willing to get in the wheelbarrow?" At that point everyone became unsure of just how much they trusted him. Yet one little boy in a red shirt raised his hand. The man said, "You! You in the red shirt! Come up here." The little boy went up, got in the wheelbarrow, and the man pushed it to the other side with him in it. Afterward, the boy came down and the crowd astonishingly asked him, "How could you trust that man to keep your life?" The boy replied, "Well, he's my father."

Love and trust are inseparable.

"BECAUSE LAWLESSNESS IS INCREASED, MOST PEOPLE'S LOVE WILL GROW COLD." (MATTHEW 24:12)

Our lack of trust is really a lack of love. The more we love Him, the more our trust grows. This passage in Matthew shows us that what's happening in the world has its arrow pointed at our love and trust in Jesus.

You may think, *I don't see how they correlate.* When the world gets darker and darker, and wickedness begins to spread, and all of the mentalities, thoughts and multiplicities start to press upon men's minds, people will lose their attention on Christ, forget His beauty and, through loss of love-exchange with Him, no longer trust Him. It can even happen in the church. Only those who hide in Him will have their love protected. But for those who do not hide in Him, *their love will wax cold.* Be assured of this. It will affect their value system and the way they live their lives.

Have you watched somebody fall in love with Jesus, but later, they simply don't follow the Lord anymore? I have many friends like this. I want to issue a caution about this business: be careful, because the devil has aimed his arrows at your love relationship with Jesus. It's the very thing he wants to take from you. If he gets that, you will grow dim, cold, dry, numb and stale. You will stop experiencing appearances of the Spirit and you will have no habitation. But if you have love, you have all of these things guaranteed.

The reason Jesus wants our love is because love makes a bond that is unbreakable. Your commitment can wane. Have you felt your resolve dissolve? That's the one thing I've learned about resolve, it always dissolves, but in surrender, you'll never cease to enter.

"FOR LOVE, A MAN WILL GIVE UP ALL THAT HE HAS."

So love makes a bond unbreakable, though other things may wane, *"love is as strong as death"* (Song of Solomon 8:6). The Bible shows us, in Song of Solomon 8, that love is even greater than riches. For it, a man will give up all he has. Yes, Christ shows us that a man will give everything over for love. We will not dishonor our Bridegroom by our wayward eye. I encourage you, put your hand on your heart and say:

"Jesus, I will not dishonor You with a wayward eye. I'm not going to look at myself, others, riches, success or even my own garment."

Can you imagine a bride who's about to get married and all she talks to you about is her dress? Can you imagine a bride walking down the aisle to her groom and all she's doing is looking at her own dress? She's so preoccupied with her dress that she doesn't even look at her groom at the end of the altar. This has happened in a lot of people's spiritual lives. They are looking only at their righteous acts; intoxicated with their own name and great feats for God, yet He sits alone in the gardens of love, longing to be longed for.

We say, "Lord, look at all these things I do for You. The garment I made for You." An important piece of information is that the garment isn't something you sew together. In a Middle-Eastern wedding, the garment was provided by the groom. As a matter of fact, not only was the bride's garment provided by the groom, but everybody in the entire ceremony had their garments provided by the groom as well.

"THE DANGER OF THE BRIDAL MOVEMENT IS THAT
MANY HAVE ONLY ADOPTED THE LANGUAGE."

This is why, when the man is found in the wedding feast not wearing the right clothes, he's cast out, because he had on a garment that wasn't provided by the groom. You don't want to show up at the marriage supper wearing a garment that you made for the simple reason that you rejected the one He provided.

As I've said before, *the danger of the bridal movement is that many have only adopted the language.* Being a bride means loss of self. The two shall no longer be two but one. It's the loss of self in another. So, if we're talking about marital things and bridal realities and we're still alive, we know nothing of bridal things. If we are self-obsessed, self-absorbed and self-centered, these things have got to go if we're going to enter into marriage.

You see, this is where we see if we are really a bride: the people will eat of the fruit of our person. Your earthly spouse is the first to know of your marriage to your heavenly spouse. Your family will see that you've lost yourself in finding Him. We can say we've lost ourselves in finding Him, but our workplace really knows our character.

We can say Jesus is number one to us, and we all would say that, but the reality is, our calendar will testify more truly than our mouth. We can't merely *say* that we're brides; we've got to be in love. It's love and marriage. Love and marriage go together like a horse and carriage. This I tell you, brother, you can't have one without the other. It's just not possible.

"HE WHO LOVES FATHER OR MOTHER MORE THAN ME IS NOT WORTHY OF ME; AND HE WHO LOVES SON OR DAUGHTER MORE THAN ME IS NOT WORTHY OF ME."
(MATTHEW 10:37)

Women, do you want to marry a man who is more in love with his mommy than you? No. You want to marry a man who loves you. Men, do you want to marry a woman who retains a love for her ex-boyfriends? No. You want to be her one and only. Jesus is saying the same thing. He's saying, *if you want to marry Me, then love Me. If you want Me to be your Bridegroom, then let Me be your Bridegroom. Don't tell Me you want to marry Me when you love everybody else more than Me. Don't tell Me you want to marry Me when you still have love in your heart for these other things.*

Jesus goes on to say, *"He who does not take his cross and follow after Me is not worthy of Me"* (Matthew 10:38). Jesus only receives exclusive love.

You can tell if your love needs revival because you start feeling numb. You start feeling like your ears are muffled. You start feeling like your heart is hard, even heartless. You start feeling like the Word of God has lost its luster. You start feeling lethargic. The name of Jesus becomes stale in your mouth. Truths that used to make your heart flutter have little to no effect on you anymore. You start to scream out in prayer because the gentle-nearness has become foreign to you.

A. B. Simpson said, "Men who raise their voices must live far away from Him." No matter how amazing the experiences we've had in the past, we need a fresh inflow of the life of God to keep them real to us.

"I'D RATHER FEEL CONTRITION [OF HEART] THAN KNOW
HOW TO DEFINE IT." —THOMAS À KEMPIS

Many of us can define bridal theology, but we no longer feel it. Perhaps, as you read this, you are crying out for marriage to the Lord. Your heart seems to cry...

"Marry me
Please, be all to me
I cannot be what I need to be
I have not ears to hear nor eyes to see
I'm broken by sin in me
Distant from real joy and peace
I have internal wars that never cease
I'm buried in life's miseries
I'm blinded to holy mysteries
I'm outside of Your victories
I want to love You now endlessly
So come and rescue me
My love, come marry me"

With this heart cry, the Lord turns around to us.

"Marry Me
Let Me be all to thee
None can be what I can be
Give ears to hear and eyes to see
Thrill your soul with ecstasy
Fill your heart with joy and peace
Make internal wars to cease
Bring you into My victories
Lift you above life's miseries
Take you into My mysteries
Love you now and endlessly
and marry you eternally."

"IF ANY MAN LOVE MY FATHER WILL LOVE HIM...AND WE WILL MAKE OUR ABODE WITH HIM." (JOHN 14:23)

The summation of this entire booklet is this: man and God are looking for each other. Man looks for fulfillment and God looks to fulfill. Herein, man finds the loss of himself in another. This is the essence of what marriage looks like. If you want to have your love for Jesus ever-increasing, you can't make it happen by human effort.

Charles Spurgeon once said, "You can't chip an iceberg into a river. But if you let it bask in the beams of the sun, the rivers will begin to flow." Realizing that loving Him is so important, the core of life, we must also remember that we cannot make ourselves love Jesus. We can't thaw ourselves into rivers of love. But if we will just bask in His beams, we will become streams and realize that He is the fulfillment of all our dreams.

MEET THE AUTHOR

Eric William Gilmour is the founder of *Sonship International*—a ministry seeking to bring the church into a deeper experience of God's presence in their daily lives. He enjoys writing on the revelation of Jesus Christ in the Scriptures and personal experience of God. He lives in Florida with his wife Brooke and their two daughters.

DISCOVER MORE AT:

🌐 **sonship-international.org**

NOTES

Made in the USA
Coppell, TX
09 May 2025

49176713R00038